Christian *Mentoring* in Recovery

By
PASTOR FRANCIS HASSETT

Copyright © 2014 by Pastor Francis Hassett

Christian Mentoring in Recovery
by Pastor Francis Hassett

Printed in the United States of America

ISBN 9781498410182

All rights reserved solely by the author. The author guarantees all contents are original and do not infringe upon the legal rights of any other person or work. No part of this book may be reproduced in any form without the permission of the author. The views expressed in this book are not necessarily those of the publisher.

Scripture quotations taken from the Holy Bible, New International Version (NIV). Copyright © 1973, 1978, 1984, 2011 by Biblica, Inc.™. Used by permission. All rights reserved.

www.xulonpress.com

This book is dedicated to God.
I would like to thank my wife Yajaira
for her support, constant prayers
and always sticking by me.

PROLOGUE

Drug and alcohol addiction is now at its highest point. It is not just an American problem. It is a problem worldwide. The OAS (Organization of American States), shows on its website that drug use in Argentina, Bolivia, Chile, Ecuador, Peru and Uruguay is increasing at an alarming rate. Drug addiction is a problem everywhere. One of the fastest growing industries in Mexico is drug rehabilitation centers. It is time for the Body of Christ to begin to get more involved. We have to start interceding through prayer and meditation to ask God if sponsoring a recovering addict is something we must do. It is not easy to deal with people who are going through drug or alcohol recovery, but I think this is exactly where God wants us to be.

Psalm 82:4 *"Rescue the weak and needy; deliver them from the hand of the wicked. "*

I always think of Mother Teresa and the work she did for the lepers and the poor of Calcutta. She was one of those soldiers that wanted to do battle from the trenches, right in the middle of the battlefield. We need more Mother Teresa's in drug and alcohol recovery. God tells us that He loves everyone. We should also.

John 3:16 *"For God so loved the world that He gave His only begotten Son, that whosoever believeth in him should not perish but have eternal life."*

TABLE OF CONTENTS

Introduction ix

Chapter 1: 13
Mentee Must Be a Born Again Christian

Chapter 2: 25
God Must Be at the Center of the Recovery Process

Chapter 3: 34
Mentee's Involvement Must Be Voluntary

Chapter 4: 42
There Must Be Commitment

Chapter 5: 50
Family/Close Friends Must Be Involved

Chapter 6: 62
Surroundings Must Change

Chapter 7: 72
The Scriptures Give Us Life to Sustain Our Sobriety

Chapter 8: 81
Through Christ, Our Past Is Forgiven

Chapter 9: 90
The Fear of God

Conclusion. 99
References 101
Glossary 103

INTRODUCTION

The concept of Christian Mentorship for recovery is not something that you find in every church. The mentorship process is a method that involves time, patience and understanding. There has to be an awareness of where this person came from, that is recovering from drug or alcohol abuse. When Jesus stopped near the well and started talking to the Samaritan woman, He was aware of where this woman came from. Jesus not only knew where she physically came from, but also her personal story.

John 4:17 *"I have no husband," she replied. Jesus said to her, "You are right when you say you have no husband. "*

Jesus told us we have to go and make disciples. **Matthew 28:19** *"Therefore go and make disciples of all nations, baptizing them in the name of the Father and of the Son and of the Holy Spirit,"*

Making disciples is not an easy process. In order to make the disciples, you have to equip them so that they become a disciple. Christian Mentorship is included in the disciple process. God has called us to help these recovering addicts. God has equipped us to help these brothers and sisters that are in need. God commands us to help them and to breathe life into their lives. **Ezekiel 37:5** *"This is what the Sovereign LORD says to these bones: I will make breath enter you, and you will come to life."*

There is a great army waiting to be mentored. This army of great and loyal soldiers will make The Body of Christ into a greater force. Let's accept the challenge. **Ezekiel 37:10** *"So I prophesied as he commanded* *me, and breath entered them; they came to life and stood up on their feet—a vast army."*

Chapter 1

ADDICT MUST BE BORN AGAIN CHRISTIAN

Isaiah 35:8 *"And a highway will be there; it will be called the Way of the Holiness. The unclean will not journey on it; it will be for those who walk in that way; wicked fools will not go about on it."*

The "Highway" to sobriety is best explained here by the prophet Isaiah. There is a road to recovery and on that road; the people who are going to help you will be born again Christians. The support you are going to need is going to come from the Body of Christ. Isaiah received a great revelation here. The road to recovery, redemption, healing, salvation etc. is filled with the Righteous who do everything through *"Jesus Highway."*

Bible.org on Isaiah 35:8: "This same metaphor of a royal visit is used to describe the coming of the Messiah…… This is a metaphor for preparation of a physical road, but it has spiritual implications referring to repentance."

The road to recovery has repentance involved in it as Bible.org helps us realize through their interpretation of Isaiah 35:8. It also involves confessions of sin and believing that Jesus is Lord and came to save us from eternal death.

Romans 10:9, 10 *"That if you confess with your mouth "Jesus is Lord", and believe in your heart that God raised Him from the dead, you will be saved. For it is with your heart that you believe and are justified, and it is with your mouth that you confess and are saved."*

Helping the recovery process with a Christian mentor involves only people who are born again Christians. The Apostle Paul emphasizes here the point that it must be something that comes from your heart. If it's not something that comes from your heart there is no commitment. Both the mentor and mentee have to be committed Christians that strive for a righteous life.

Disciples of Christ are responsible for teaching the new disciples on how to live a righteous life *IN CHRIST*. At the same time that it is through Christ that we do this, it is with the help of Christ that we can accomplish this mentorship.

Matthew 28:20 *"Teach these new disciples to obey all the commands I have given you. And be sure of this: I am with you always, even to the end of the age."*

The greatest part about all this is that through the redemption we received from Jesus' sacrifice for us on the cross; we receive grace and mercy that helps sustain us through this process.

Ephesians 2:4,5 *"But because of His great love for us, God, who is rich in mercy, made us alive with Christ even when we were dead in transgressions – it is by grace you have been saved."*

Because a committed born again Christian has grace and mercy built into their consistency, it helps the recovering mentee in the healing process, which is needed in order to move forward in a full recovery.

John 3:5-8 *"Jesus answered, "I tell you the truth, no one can enter the kingdom of God unless he is born of water and the Spirit. Flesh gives birth to flesh, but the Spirit of gives birth to Spirit. You should not be surprised at my saying 'you must be born again'. The wind blows wherever it pleases. You hear its sound but you cannot tell where it comes from or where* *it is going. So it is with everyone born of the Spirit."*

Being born again is a spiritual thing that involves us relying on things that we cannot see. Our help that we start to receive is not something tangible that we can see and touch. Convincing someone that our journey through this is going to be with the help of someone that we can't see is tough. This is where faith steps in and takes over some of those doubts.

2 Samuel 22:26 *"To the faithful you show yourself faithful, to the blameless you show yourself blameless "*

The mentee must keep building their faith up. This is one of the most difficult processes. They have to go to the scriptures to keep building that faith up.

Romans 10:17 *"Consequently, faith comes from hearing the message, and the message is heard through the word of Christ."*

Relying on recovery help from secular places is not always the best way to go. I think there are some steps that work in these secular programs. Narcotics Anonymous and Alcoholics Anonymous both use some type of 12 step system. There is some faith-based steps involved, but God is not the main focus. We come to a realization that all knowledge comes from God for a reason.

Proverbs 2:6 *"For the Lord gives wisdom, and from his mouth comes knowledge and understanding."*

There are probably many people who have had success using these systems. The reason I think a faith based, God centered, mentor program works best is because the results are different. I have personally seen 12 step graduates finish these programs and not go back to using drugs or alcohol, but their life still seemed empty. I personally had the opportunity to mentor a recovering addict. This man, who we will call "Milton" was mentored not only by me, but by other believers. "Milton's" life now, through the mentoring process, is a dramatic change from when he first started this process. He went from being an addict in the streets to a God fearing husband of two children. The contrast from before and after is amazing. He now has a youth ministry in his church and is training to be a Pastor. I spent two years with him in this mentoring process. Before he started working with me he had been a born again believer for about two years. We both did not realize how important it was that serving Christ and being a born-again Christian was the key to a successful mentorship. A big part of mentoring was the example that I set with my daily life. We both worked at the same job, attended the same church. Everywhere that he saw me, he saw the same person. Christ was the answer to his problems and changing his old ways of being. It was Christ that I wanted him to see through me and my actions. **CHRIST** is the one who was going to set him free.

Galatians 5:1 *"It is for freedom that Christ has set us free, stand firm then & do not let yourself be burdened again by a yoke of slavery."*

One thing I realized is that people that come from the "street" respect other people that come from the "street." "Milton" knew where I came from and my history of drug addiction. He saw the transformation in my life. He saw that it was okay to be a Christian and let go of those old ways of being. You don't have to act tough any more. He saw that it's good to worship God, that it's good to read the bible and talk about it, it's good to be around your family and dedicate yourself to them. All these things please God and he saw it from someone that came from the same place he did. This mentoring process is not something that happens overnight. It takes time, patience, love and a lot of help from above.

Galatians 5:22, 23" *But the fruit of the spirit is love, joy, peace, patience, kindness, goodness, faithfulness, gentleness and self-control. Against such things there is no law."*

It basically comes down to this: the mentee has to see results. Where he can see genuine fruits of the spirit manifested, from whoever is mentoring him/her.

I read an article on the internet it was from a blog that is mainly visited by recovering addicts who are Christian. There was one blog from a Reverend Dr. Paul Bradley who is one of the board members of the New York Theological Seminary. In it he writes:

"In his second letter to the Corinthians (12:9) the Apostle Paul tells us that "power is made perfect in weakness."

Sometimes this line is translated as my strength is made perfect in weakness. This central message of our Christian faith is also essential to the very survival of people in recovery from addictions, compulsions and destructive behaviors, attitudes and relationships. It starts with step one. We admit our powerlessness over the substance, behaviors, attitudes and relationships that drag us down, destroying our spirits, our lives and our very essence. Paul captures this great human quandary well in Romans 7:19 *"For I do not do the good I want, but the evil I do not want is what I do.* "Surrendering, defeated, we are finally able to say "God I am weak. I am power-less. Paul explains in 2 Corinthians that we can be boastful and feel elated, but to keep us from ever being too high on ourselves, we're given thorns in our flesh – a message from satan or perhaps, what we might describe today as visitations from "our personal demons". We pray to God to remove these thorns to free us from "our demons." In Paul we read that power is made perfect in weakness, in order for us to be filled with Christ, we must be weak. This is the seeming contradiction embedded in our relationship with God, and in addition and recovery. To have the strength to live free of demonizing influence, we must let go absolutely, surrendering everything and let God's love fill us, melt us, mold us, and transform us. At the moment we hit bottom, as we finally admit we are powerless and can't do it by ourselves anymore, we attain our moment of greatest strength out of the depths of despair. Out of weakness, comes the ultimate transfigured and transcendent strength. Christian fellowship at its heart empowers us to open the doorways and windows of our

hearts, minds and souls, letting God's love and light flood our lives."

Reverend Bradley, along with support from the scriptures, fortifies what I've been saying in this chapter. There has to be surrender. This process is continued through fellowship and mentoring with other born again believers.

Chapter 2

GOD MUST BE AT THE CENTER OF THE RECOVERY PROCESS

Proverbs 19:21 *"Many are the plans in a man's heart but it is the Lord's purpose that prevails."*

Most addicts should take this verse and keep it in their heart. There is a connection between addiction and self-centeredness. When the addict is going through the recovery process, they still have that selfishness that they take with them. That selfishness is always there throughout their recovery process. Because of this mindset, it is difficult it is difficult to refocus and learn to put your trust in other people, let alone God. While in addiction the focus is where that next high is coming from. Most don't care how they'll get the money to get those drugs. I'll never forget what a friend once told me:" when it comes to money to get high, you can never trust another addict, but when it comes to getting money together to get something to eat you can depend on them. Addicts don't let other addicts starve, but when it comes to drugs forget it. "This just proves to me that it was the drugs and the addiction that bring about the selfishness.

Isaiah 45:6, 7- *"so that from the rising of the sun to the place of its setting men may know there is none besides me. I am the Lord, and there is no other. I form the light and created darkness, I bring prosperity and create disaster; I, the Lord do all these things. "*

The prophet Isaiah here shows us that God that really is in the middle of everything, through your addiction, through your recovery, through your sobriety, God is always there.

We are just too self-centered to realize that God was always trying to get our attention. I always look back at where God took me out from, just to think about how blind I was. I was stuck in the middle of a bad cycle. Doing drugs, doing what I had to do to get drugs. I did not know how to get out of doing all this crazy stuff. Because God was not at the center of my life, everything just kept going wrong. To get to the point where God is at the center right in the middle, right in your face, something dramatic has to happen. Without that big dramatic thing happening to make you change, it's going to be tough.

Jeremiah 29:11" *for I know the plans I have for you" declares the Lord, plans to prosper you and not harm you, and plans to give you hope and a future."*

The Lord knows what he wants to do with you and your future. The only one holding you back is you. When God says that He does not want to*" harm you"*, it's because He really wants no harm done to you. In other words He is trying to convince you that he has nothing to do with what you are doing to yourself. His plans are for good, not for bad. When God is not at the center of your life, your focus is you and what you can do to get yourself out of your predicament. This selfishness brings almost like an arrogance that makes you feel like if YOU can't get yourself of it, than N0 ONE can. This is why a lot of the 12 steppers a lot of times don't go through the whole process and afterward leave the program. They feel that they can either finish the process by them self or that they can do a better 12 step program on their own.

Matthews 19:26" *With man this is impossible. But with God all things are possible."*

Recovery, completely on our terms, does not get full 100% results. Getting your mind to completely grasp the idea: that the key to a victorious life, is to give your everything and surrender to God; is not an easy thing to do. It's a gradual process that the disciple takes to completely understand what Jesus was trying to teach them.

Matthew 13:36" *Then he left the crowd and went into the house. His disciples come to him and said" Explain to us the parable of the weeds in the fields."*

The disciples' ministry did not completely start until Jesus ascended to heaven. Like I was saying earlier, something dramatic had to happen in order for them to get started completely with what they had to do.

Job 12:9, 10, *"which of all these does not know that the hand of the Lord has done this? In His hand is the life of every creature and the breath of all mankind."*

When God is at the center of recovery, or anything else for that matter, there has to be results. I have the privilege of knowing a brother and sister of mine that run a Christian recovery house. These two servants of the Lord have great big hearts that love God and do everything they can to get these addicts to change their lives. They do what they can, but one thing they can't do, is change a person's heart. If God is not truly the center of your life, you're not really getting anywhere. Most of these guys don't really have a place to go, they've hit rock bottom, so they just go to a recovery house and act like they are repenting. You know that there heart is not truly in it, because they spend 2 or 3 years in the program and nothing comes out of it. They either just go back to using drugs or go to another program. They do whatever they have to do to stay off the streets. We know their heart is not really in it, and the results tell you everything.

Mathews 7:17" *likewise every good tree bears good fruit, but a bad tree bears bad fruit."*

Proverbs 16:9" *in his heart a man plans his cause, but the Lord determines his steps."*

Up there in heaven, God probably has the biggest room that you can imagine. It is bigger than the planet earth. He probably has a team of thousands and thousands of angels

God Must Be At The Center of The Recovery Process

---

that work in this room. In this room he has video and audio of all the thoughts and whatever that goes through our mind. I'm making this up, I think, but if this were true, can we even imagine all the things that we planned and schemed in our heads. Everything that we wanted to accomplish. How many times did we put at the beginning of the thought "what would God think of this" or Does God want this for my life. Remember, God has all the footage on your answers. Working with a mentee. It is crucial that we know for certain that he/she has God at the center of their plans to get them through this time of change. In order to bring real changes, there has to be a real sense of depending on God to get them through their time of need.

1 Corinthians 10:13"*No temptations have seized you except what is common to man. And God is faithful; he will not let you be tempted, He will also provide a way out so that you can stand up under it.*"

If God is in it, and you voluntarily let him let him be in it, how can you go wrong? He makes sure that there's always a solution to how you can get out of certain circumstances. Of course you have to do your part, there's no way around it. I know that free will is a subject that most theologians don't agree on, one way or another, but I think that recovery itself, gives a strong case for God giving us some free will. How many "potential ministers of the Lord" are still out there in the streets doing drugs? I don't know. There are other factors involved in the mentoring process. It's long and complicated but if you don't give it all to God, how can it be done? I think there are many ministers out there who just have not gotten over their selfishness and just given their complete trust to the Lord. Remember that in 1 Cor 10:13, God is talking to his faithful servants, the ones who have given him their complete trust and are going through certain trials and tribulations.

Psalms 37:23" *if the Lord delights in man's way, he makes his steps firm.*"

God has to see you making strides towards his way. A recovering addict has to be on solid ground in the process and God is the only one to make it happen.

Chapter 3

MENTEE'S INVOLVEMENT MUST BE VOLUNTARY

Philemon 1:14" *But I did not want to do anything without your consent, so that any favor you do will be spontaneous and not forced.*"

I think it is a noble thing when someone goes into recovery, because a loved one asked them to. The only problem I see with this, is that it really doesn't get to the root of the problem. The mentee is solving the loved ones problem, not his/her own issues. Don't get me wrong, this could be a good way to get them in the right direction, but there is still work to do afterwards. There is a woman that I know who has a daughter addicted to drugs. She is constantly trying to get her daughter to get into a recovery program. Her daughter just does not want to stop. She says she enjoys getting high. The mother cannot force her own will into her daughter's heart. Her daughter just doesn't want to stop. The mother's only real option is to intercede through prayer and ask God for a break through.

Psalms 119:105" *your word is a lamp to my feet and a light to my Path.*"

Deuteronomy 23:23" *whatever your lips utter you must be sure to do, because you made your vow freely to the Lord your God with your own mouth.*"

Webster's Dictionary defines voluntary as follows:" brought about by one's own free choice" In this definition, and I'm pretty sure any other definition by other dictionaries, it says nothing about a second person involved. There is only the free will of the person who is going to get started in the recovery process. I know that there are a lot of times people might think that because you don't keep insisting or persisting with the person to get started on the road to recovery that you don't have compassion. I think compassion has nothing to do with it. Like I said earlier, you can't force your will unto anyone. Even Jesus didn't force the Gospel on anyone.

Matthews 10:14" *whoever does not receive you, nor heed your words, as you go out of the house or that city, shake the dust off your feet."*

Psalm 54:6 *"willingly I will sacrifice to you; I will give thanks to your name, o Lord for it is good."*

David did not get to this point because anyone told him to. It was a gradual process that took him from herding sheep to being King. God anointed him and he believed it from a young age. He willingly, over time just kept believing more and more that God was behind him in all he did and he was going to accomplish everything God set him out to do.

1 Samuel 16:12, 13"*So he sent and had him brought in. He was ruddy, with a fine appearance and handsome features. Then the Lord said, 'Rise and anoint him; he is the one.' So Samuel took the horn of oil and anointed him in the presence of his brothers, and from that day on the Spirit of the Lord came upon David in power. Samuel then went to Ramah.*"

When Samuel came to Jesse's house, the only thing Samuel did was to anoint David. He didn't go there to give David instructions. David had to voluntarily fulfill his destiny.

Exodus 35:29"*All the Israelite men and women who were willing brought to the Lord freewill offerings for all the work the Lord has through Moses had commanded them to do.*"

The things of God involve work. Work involves a desire to do something. Without that desire, your will to do something is not there. The desire in your heart has to overcome whatever is blocking your mind. This mental blockage that comes from whatever reason must be overcome. The Israelites spent 40 years in the desert and never overcame this mental blockage. These people infected Moses with their way of thinking. Moses had no choice sometimes but to let them do what they wanted.

Matthew 19:7-8" why then, "they asked, "did Moses command that a man give his wife a certificate of divorce and send her away?"

"Jesus replied, "Moses permitted you to divorce your wife's because your hearts were hard. But it was not this way from the beginning."

The Israelites did not want to do anything voluntarily. So God let them do what they wanted and let them die in the dessert. If there is no voluntary action taken to better your life, you're just going to stay stuck.

Luke 15:10 *"in the same way, I tell you, there is joy in the presence of the angels of God over one sinner who repents."*

Mentee's Involvement Must Be Voluntary

Recovery involves people who have used drugs, alcohol, etc. for a period of time and are trying to stop using the drugs, alcohol, etc. The effects of abusing the brain and body with these substances is not 100% known. The only things I can say is that it probably makes changes in your normal way of being. Whatever substance is being abused, takes over your body and probably causes a chemical imbalance. The drug becomes a top priority to your body and it takes over your mind, body and soul. The chemical imbalance is a part of why its' so hard for the addict to submit.

James 4:7 *"Submit therefore to God, resist the devil and he will flee you."*

2 Chronicles 12:14 *"He did evil because he had not set his heart on seeking the Lord."*

It's a very difficult process for anyone to do anything without God. I say it from a Christian perspective. Whenever I am about to take a project or start something, I just have a hard time with it if I don't take it to God first.

Matthews 6:33"*but seek first the kingdom of and His righteousness, and all these things will be given to you as well.*"

The statistics on a full, healthy recovery for brothers/sisters coming out of a Christian recovery house is staggering. Out of every 50 coming out if these recovery maybe 1 or 2 make a good, strong recovery. The main reason is that there is no real voluntary commitment to the process. You have to submit and admit that you are helpless. Whatever the reason, whether its ego, stubbornness, or whatever the case may be, you just have to overcome these and put them aside.

Isaiah 2:7-8"*Their land is full of silver and gold; there is no end to their treasures. Their land is full of horses; there is no end to their chariots. Their land is full of idols; they bow down to the work of their hands, to what their fingers have made.*"

Selfish behavior brings about an inward thought process. Just like the prophet Isaiah tells us here in this verse. We start thinking about what we can do on our own. Getting into a recovery program and sticking with it, are the first steps you have to take. Christian mentoring is something that comes after recovery. And mostly by this time, the road is lonely. It's a personal journey, and the next steps after you recover are steps that you make on your own. You are starting out fresh. It's like when you are lost in the wilderness. You don't know where you are at but you have to make that first move. You can't just sit down and do nothing, your survival depends on you making the first step and making something happen.

Isaiah 50:11 *"But now, all you who lights fire and provide yourself with flaming torches, go, walk in the light of your fires and of the torches you have set ablaze. This is what you shall receive from my hand; you will lie down in torment."*

Chapter 4

THERE MUST BE COMMITMENT

Psalm 37:5" *Commit your way to the Lord, trust in him. And he will do this"*

Commitment to do anything is probably something that most of us deal with on a daily basis. We can try to make commitments to our family, friends, work, school, etc. Making the commitment and actually being committed are the two different things. I can make a commitment to bring my wife a flower every day. That's a big commitment if I don't actually bring the flower every day to my wife; I'm not actually accomplishing what I committed to. I have to think about what is reasonable and make a commitment to something obtainable. I now commit to bringing my wife a flower once every Friday. This is a reasonable commitment I can accomplish, and I'm now fulfilling what I intended to do.

Philippians 3:12-14" *Not that I have already obtained all this, or have already been made perfect, but I press on to take hold of that for which Christ Jesus took hold of me. Brothers, I do not consider myself yet to have taken hold of it. But one thing I do: Forgetting what is behind and straining toward what is ahead, I press on toward the goal to win the prize for which God has called me heavenward in Christ Jesus."*

The Apostle Paul tells us here that our zeal or passion for whatever we have committed to should always be the same. A commitment to do something involves being in it with all your heart. I think the Apostle Paul mentions this here because he realizes that we sometimes just either get caught up with emotions or our heart is not in it.

**Psalm 19:*14* **"*May these words of my mouth and this meditation of my heart be pleasing in your sight, Lord, my rock and my Redeemer.*"

Whatever the words are that come out of my mouth; they have to match up with what I feel in my heart and the results that come from it.

Psalm 119:5 "*oh that my ways were steadfast in obeying your decrees.*"

We have to realize that the main reason we have to be committed is because without commitment, it's hard to listen to the voice of God. If our heart is not in it, we are only listening to our own thoughts and doubts like the Psalmist David tells us here, we have to be "Steadfast" in pursuing what God tells us to do. There is commitment here and it's not a small one. When it comes to God and what he needs and requires of us is no small task. Some people probably don't believe that there is work involved in serving God. I think one of the most misquoted verses that people apply to this, is in the book of Matthews.

Matthews 11:30 *"For my yoke is easy and my burden is light."*

Jesus was talking about the burden of those who wore not born again. They believed in other things that put a burden on them like what the Pharisees and Sadducees taught. There were many requirements and laws that were impossible to keep up with. With Jesus in our life, we are not under all these unattainable responsibilities. His Grace is sufficient.

2 Corinthians 12:9, 10 *"But he said to me, "My grace is sufficient for you, for my power is made perfect in weakness." Therefore I will boast all the more gladly about my weaknesses, so that Christ's power may rest on me. ¹⁰ That is why, for Christ's sake, I delight in weaknesses, in insults, in hardships, in persecutions, in difficulties. For when I am weak, then I am strong."*

1 Peter 2:25 *"For you were like sheep going astray," but now you have returned to the Shepherd and Overseer of your souls."*

Being mentored will make the most sense when we give our full attention to God. There can't be a good relationship between a mentor and a mentee without that full commitment between both of them and God. Moving forward without this is not an option. I can think back and wonder what if I did not obligate myself to dedicating my life to God. I and my family would not be at this point in our lives without feeling the obligation to serve God. The mentees mind has to be filled with the sense of purpose and goals to be accomplished.

Philippians 3:14 *"I press on toward the goal to win the prize for which God has called me heavenward in Christ Jesus."*

1 Peter 3:13" Who is going to harm you if you are eager to do good?"

With God on our side and good intentions in your heart there is only a good path in front of you. Setting goals and achieving them is a good start. Even if it is small goals that you start with. Knowing that you set out to do something and it happened, is a good motivator. The human mind is something that, in order for it to be used properly, needs to be activated. This activation is done through what you tell it to do. It's like a computer that that needs for it to be input with its commands. I don't really think there is a 100% complete understanding of how the mind, along with your brain, work together to accomplish anything. It is one of the wonders that God has given us. It's through this process that we succeed in our lives.

Job 11:13-15 *"Yet if you devote your heart to him and stretch out your hands to him, if you put away the sin that is in your hand and allow no evil to dwell in your tent, then, free of fault, you will lift up your face; you will stand firm and without fear."*

Purpose in life and objectives need to be put in front of us in order to get anywhere. The carrot in front of the rabbit, the cheese in front of the mouse, these things dangling in front are something we all need. They are motivating factors that keep us moving. Self-esteem can sometimes be a reason why we never set certain goals. We just don't think that certain scenarios are for us. I sometimes look at certain people and their accomplishments and think, "That's not for me, and it's not within my capabilities." And that'll be the end of that. I didn't set that goal of doing what that certain person is doing because I didn't think I was within my capacity, and that's it, the idea died. We have to motivate the mentee sometimes to feel like they are capable, that it is within their capabilities to accomplish anything.

Philippians 4:13 *"I can do all this through him who gives me strength."*

Psalms 31:5 *"Into your hands I commit my spirit; deliver me, LORD, my faithful God."*

With God involved, there is truth. The true feelings of your heart and the desires of your heart are revealed when God is involved in the process. With God involved comes His purpose and we always have to keep this in mind. At the end of the road is going to come what God has intended for our lives. Commitment to God first brings an easier way to commit to anything else in our life.

Chapter 5

FAMILY / CLOSE FRIENDS MUST BE INVOLVED

Luke 15:13-24 *"Not long after that, the younger son got together all he had, set off for a distant country and there squandered his wealth in wild living. After he had spent everything, there was a severe famine in that whole country, and he began to be in need. So he went and hired himself out to a citizen of that country, who sent him to his fields to feed pigs. He longed to fill his stomach with the pods that the pigs were eating, but no one gave him anything."*

"When he came to his senses, he said, 'How many of my father's hired servants have food to spare, and here I am starving to death! I will set out and go back to my father and say to him: Father, I have sinned against heaven and against you. I am no longer worthy to be called your son; make me like one of your hired servants.' So he got up and went to his father.

"But while he was still a long way off, his father saw him and was filled with compassion for him; he ran to his son, threw his arms around him and kissed him.

"The son said to him, 'Father, I have sinned against heaven and against you. I am no longer worthy to be called your son.'

"But the father said to his servants, 'Quick! Bring the best robe and put it on

him. Put a ring on his finger and sandals on his feet. Bring the fattened calf and kill it. Let's have a feast and celebrate. For this son of mine was dead and is alive again; he was lost and is found.' So they began to celebrate. "

The story of the prodigal son is one of the most quoted stories in the bible. Jesus used this parable to explain how God looks at those who repent and turn to Jesus for their forgiveness of sin. I think this parable is valid in this case because of the way the family is portrayed. The younger son wanted to take his inheritance and leave home. He spent everything and came back home broken and broke. With the help of his father, he was restored to how he was before. Even though he came back home with different experiences that he went through, his father still accepted him. What the younger son experienced and experimented with changed his life forever. His mindset was different. He no longer looked at the world through adolescent eyes. It says here in the story that he spent his inheritance on "wild living." Everything in this story has parallels with the lives of recovering addicts. At the end of the story, the father accepts his son with open arms. It is through the help of his father, family and friends that he is accepted and brought back into the family. During the celebration all the family was rejoicing. This means that the family was there to get the young son through his healing process. The older brother was not too happy about the happy welcome that the younger brother received. This older brother represents the obstacles that get in the way of a full recovery.

Matthew 2:13-15 *"When they had gone, an angel of the Lord appeared to Joseph in a dream. "Get up," he said, "take the child and his mother and escape to Egypt. Stay there until I tell you, for Herod is going to search for the child to kill him." So he got up, took the child and his mother during the night and* *left for Egypt, where he stayed until the death of Herod. And so was fulfilled what the Lord had said through the prophet: "Out of Egypt I called my son."*

What happened here in this story of Joseph and Mary is a true testament to a family persevering together. God sent an angel to Joseph to convince him that it was necessary for him to be a part of the birth of Jesus.

Matthew 1:20 *"But after he had considered this, an angel of the Lord appeared to him in a dream and said, "Joseph son of David, do not be afraid to take Mary home as your wife, because what is conceived in her is from the Holy Spirit."*

In order for Mary to conceive Jesus and fulfill what God has set forth to do, Joseph had to be part of the process. Joseph had to be part of it because that's how God intended the family to be.

Genesis 2:24 *"That is why a man leaves his father and mother and is united to his wife, and they become one flesh."*

The family staying together is the reason Jesus was able to be safely taken to Egypt. The family concept was always in God's plan. The family pulling together through rough times was also in God's Plan. In the mentoring process a mentee has to sit back and analyze this. Every mentees family/friend support system is different. Some mentees have no wife or kids, some do. Some have a mother, no father. Whatever the case may be, this aspect in the mentoring process is vital. Although there is a voluntary commitment that has only to do with the mentee, there is going to be help needed. Joseph took command of his family and got them to the point where their life was stabilized. When Jesus started his ministry there was no obstacles in the way. Joseph and Mary made sure he got to this point. The mentoring process is going to involve family/friends support that gets him/her to the point where their life is stabilized.

Genesis 8:15, 16 *"Then God said to Noah, "Come out of the ark, you and your wife and your sons and their wives."*

The Lord sent Noah into the ark with his family. He did not just send him by himself. It was with his family that they were going to get through this traumatic event. My drug addiction took its toll on my family. When I finally hit rock bottom my life could have gone either way. My wife and kids had every right to leave me and never come back. I was not fulfilling my role as a father. God had other plans. He touched my wife's heart and let her know that she should stay with me in order to accomplish his mission. With my wife and kids my recovery had a deeper meaning. There was purpose and hope that all would change to make our life better. Because our family stayed together, we have grown and matured as a family. It was through family support that this happened. I don't know what would have happened if I went through this process on my own.

Ezra 1:5" *Then the family heads of Judah and Benjamin, and the priests and Levites—everyone whose heart God had moved—prepared to go up and build the house of the LORD in Jerusalem.*"

The mentee is going to need the help and support of other people. There is a long road to a full recovery. And help along the way is a good thing to have. The 12 step program has sponsors for this reason. They require that you go through their program while staying in touch with a sponsor the whole way. The only difference here is that the 12 step programs emphasizes that this whole process be done alone with their sponsors. I don't think you're always guaranteed a mature sponsor. I remember my father going through an Alcoholics Anonymous program with a sponsor who had only been in the program for less than 1 year. I just think a person in recovery for less than 1 year is not ready to mentor or sponsor someone. The road to full recovery is something that takes years. Being paired up with someone else in recovery with less than one year is not a good idea. These two have the potential to relapse because of their short time being away from alcohol/drugs.

1 Timothy 3:6 *"He must not be a recent convert, or he may become conceited and fall under the same judgment as the devil."*

Joshua 6:23 *"So the young men who had done the spying went in and brought out Rahab, her father and mother and brothers and all who belonged to her. They brought out her entire family and put them in a place outside the camp of Israel."*

Throughout the bible we are always given examples on God saving families as a whole. Here we see that Rahab was the one who helped the spies, but the whole family was spared. Lot and his family were spared from the destruction of Sodom and Gomorrah when Abraham interceded for them.

Genesis 19:29 *"So when God destroyed the cities of the plain, he remembered Abraham, and he brought Lot out of the catastrophe that overthrew the cities where Lot had lived."*

All of these stories in the bible deal with families, as a whole part, going through the different circumstances. God made sure that these families, as a whole part, were together when they were going through their difficult times. This is no coincidence. God wants us to get through our struggles together as a family. There's no better guide to success than Gods Word, through the bible, to help us in difficult times. Going through every step with scriptures backing us up is the key to a successful mentorship on both sides. The mentee must come to realize that he/she plans out in his mind who they think will best help them out in this process. This is very important. A family united with one purpose is a powerful weapon.

Genesis 14:13-16" *A man who had escaped came and reported this to Abram the Hebrew. Now Abram was living near the great trees of Mamre the Amorite, a brother of Eshkol and Aner, all of whom were allied with Abram. When Abram heard that his relative had been taken captive, he called out the 318 trained men born in his household and went in pursuit as far as Dan. During the night Abram divided his men to attack them and he routed them, pursuing them as far as Hobah, north of Damascus. He recovered all the goods and brought back his relative Lot and his possessions, together with the women and the other people."*

In these verses we see that Abraham found out that his nephew was in distress. He got together all the soldiers in his family, which was about 318. The bible does not exact in telling us how many they fought against, but my guess is that there was a whole lot more of them. Abraham's men fought against the armies of 4 different kings. Abraham never put any thought into this fact. The only thing that was on his mind was that he had to get his nephew back. Abraham and his family had one purpose in their mind and they all got together and helped out his nephew.

Chapter 6

SURROUNDINGS MUST CHANGE

Psalm 1:1 *"Blessed is the one who does not walk in step with the wicked or stand in the way that sinners take or sit in the company of mockers."*

There's a good reason why God keeps warning us over and over again about the company we keep and how we have to be careful about our surroundings.

This applies in the mentorship process and is vital. Being around the wrong people or at the wrong place at the wrong time can have very bad consequences. It can make you go all the way back, not only in the mentoring process but also recovery. A certain person that I will call "John" was under a mentoring process with a friend of mine. "John" was careful about who he was around. Being careful of your environment is essential because the temptation is too great. John started hanging around with his two brothers. Remember I said that you have to choose carefully who you want around you in this process, even family. It's important to have family around you but you still have to choose wisely even with your family. If your family member is on drugs, you can't be around them. "John's" brother got him back into drugs and we didn't hear from "John" for a while. We found out that he was back on drugs and living under a bridge. "John" was found a few months later under that same bridge almost frozen to death. He passed away two weeks later. "John" started out great in the mentoring process. He was going on preaching campaigns with my friend and being a great inspiration to others. He just wasn't being careful about his environment, he fell and he fell hard.

Psalm 120:7" *I am for peace; but when I speak, they are for war."*

Matthews Henry's concise commentary says this about this verse.

"He is very grievous to a good man, to be cast into, and kept in the company of the wicked, from whom he hopes to be forever separated."

It's pretty sad to see good men try so hard to change their lives and lose everything just because they were careless for a moment. That's the thing about being in a bad environment. It sucks you in if you are not careful. Sometimes you don't even realize it.

Psalms 125:2" *As the mountains surround Jerusalem, so the LORD surrounds his people both now and forevermore."*

God wants you to be surrounded by a good team of people. David reminds us that when you are doing the things of God, He surrounds you and everything and everyone around you. He does this, considering that you are committed to making an effort to surround yourself with righteous people. God has a way of making things come to light.

Luke 8:17" *For there is nothing hidden that will not be disclosed, and nothing concealed that will not be known or brought out into the open."*

Asking God for discernment throughout this process is very important. There is no other way. My friend who fell just never realized his brothers were going to bring him down.

1 Corinthians 15:33 *"Do not be misled: "Bad company corrupts good character."*

Deuteronomy 6:14" *Do not follow other gods, the gods of the peoples around you."*

The best way to focus on this is to surround yourself with people who are on the same page as you. It's hard living in this world and staying away from temptation that you've already fallen for. If you have a sober person that has always been sober, they will probably have a good chance of not being tempted if they pass by a drug block. If you used to get high, you can't you can't pass by that same block and not get tempted. You have to not only watch your surroundings, but also the people that you are around.

Proverbs 6:27 *"Can a man scoop fire into his lap without his clothes being burned?"*

When I first got out of prison, I stayed with a friend of mine. I needed a place to stay and he did me the favor of letting me stay at his house. I was still on parole when I got out and had to get drug tested once a month. My friend smoked marijuana all day, every day. I had to leave his house because of the environment. If I had stayed, I would have come back positive for marijuana and went back to prison. Even though he is a friend of mine, the influence was not positive so I analyzed and made a decision to not be around that environment.

Surroundings Must Change

Proverbs 13:20" *Walk with the wise and become wise, for a companion of fools suffers harm."*

There has to be a conscious effort to stay away from old habits. Like the story of the prodigal son. He came back different, but he couldn't get caught up in going back to that other environment he was in. **1 Peter 5:8**" *Be alert and of sober mind. Your enemy the devil prowls around like a roaring lion looking for someone to devour."*

There has to be a conscious effort to resist staying away. Even the most suitable thing that seems harmless can trigger a relapse or worse. I sometimes get offered a beer or two and I always say no. I think that for an average person who is not an addict that is not a big deal if they have that one beer or drink. I can't. I know that even if nothing happens in that moment that it slowly but surely will lead to a big down fall. I just make it a habit of politely saying no and to keep it moving and be on my way. Sometimes that's just the best thing to do, just walk away.

1 Corinthians 5:11" *But now I am writing you that you must not associate with anyone who calls himself a brother but is sexually immoral or greedy, an idolater or a slanderer, a drunkard or a swindler. With such a man do not even eat.*"

You have to be conscious everywhere, even in church. You might see some brothers/sisters on Sunday and think that they are okay. Outside of church it might be a different story. It could be that they are only going to church out of obligation or whatever the reason. But if they are not living right, and you see this from them when they are not in church, then you have to disassociate yourself from that person. If you're trying to make a full recovery, you can't take that chance that they will be a bad influence.

1 Corinthians 6:9-10 *"Or do you not know that wrongdoers will not inherit the kingdom of God? Do not be deceived: Neither the* *sexually immoral nor idolaters nor adulterers nor men who have sex with men nor thieves nor the greedy nor drunkards nor slanderers nor swindlers will inherit the kingdom of God."*

It might seem dramatic that you go to such extremes to separate yourself from all these people. But if the mentee is going to have a successful mentorship, it must be done.

1 John 3:4" *Everyone who sins breaks the law; in fact, sin is lawlessness."*

Serving Christ is a continual cleansing process. God won't depend on us to be perfect. But since we are born again we are new in Christ.

2 Corinthians 5:17" *Therefore, if anyone is in Christ, the new creation has come: The old has gone, the new is here."*

We need to have a different mentality in order to be aware and be able to better discern your surroundings. I have four children from ages 12 to 19 years old. A lot of family members criticized me and my wife because we never let our children go anywhere without supervision. We always have to know where they are going and who they are going to be with. If we don't know either of these things, they cannot go. We do it because they are our children and we are making sure there environment is always a safe and sound one. We do it out of love, not because we are controlling.

1 John 4:8 *"Whoever does not love does not know God, because God is love."*

2 Thessalonians 3:6" *In the name of the Lord Jesus Christ, we command you, brothers and sisters, to keep away from every believer who is idle and disruptive and does not live according to the teaching you received from us."*

The mentor and mentee have to be surrounded with good people and be in a good atmosphere. Our mind works with the five senses. Any one of these senses can take us back to our old life. Passing by a certain street (where you used to cop), objects, smells associated with drug use can trigger a relapse.

1 Peter 4:3-5" *For you have spent enough time in the past doing what pagans choose to do—living in debauchery, lust, drunkenness, orgies, carousing and detestable idolatry. They are surprised that you do not join them in their reckless, wild living, and they heap abuse on you. But they will have to give account to him who is ready to judge the living and the dead.*"

Chapter 7

THE SCRIPTURES GIVE US LIFE TO SUSTAIN OUR SOBRIETY

John 1:1-5" *In the beginning was the Word, and the Word was with God, and the Word was God. He was with God in the beginning. Through him all things were made; without him nothing was made that has been made. In him was life, and that life was the light of all mankind. The light shines in the darkness, and the darkness has not overcome it.*"

The Scriptures Give Us Life To Sustain Our Sobriety

The mentee has to start establishing a regular time for prayer, reading the word, going to church and fellowship. These are like our lifeline; the answer to all our problems comes from God's word. Starting a routine with all these things I mentioned above will bring you God's word. That's how God works. I know that me personally, I have gotten most of my revelations or things I needed to hear from God from either the bible, preaching or a fellow believer. The mentee needs to start training his mind to start depending on God's word for guidance.

John 6:36" *But as I told you, you have seen me and still you do not believe."*

The words that Jesus speaks gives Life. You have to get to the point where every day you get up, you think to yourself "I need God to guide me." If that thirst for God and His Word aren't there, you need to get there. I know God uses man to deliver his message but the message comes from Him. Every day I seek God and for Him to talk to me. Whenever God gives me a reply, through whatever means He wants to use, I feel great. I feel like if He's giving me that special attention. It's this joy that we should seek whenever we feel lost. This is what is going to sustain us along with the support we get from our team. When we get into the spiritual world of God, everything changes.

Romans 16:26" *but now revealed and made known through the prophetic writings by the command of the eternal God, so that all the Gentiles might come to the obedience that comes from faith."*

All throughout the bible, God always uses his prophetic writings to guide his people from Moses with the Ten Commandments, to John in Revelations; God puts life into His Word. God does this because he can't talk to us face to face. Whenever I receive something from God, I feel it. It doesn't matter to me that I can't see Him. I know He's there.

John 1:18" *No one has ever seen God, but the one and only Son, who is himself God* *and is in closest relationship with the Father, has made him known."*

The mentee should have a relationship with God that is real and can be felt. The mentee is going to need answers and those answers are going to come through God's word. We also have to be careful, because even though God uses preaching to talk to us, the preaching has to be biblically based. Sometimes when he uses a believer, you have to make sure that what comes from that believer comes from God. It has to make sense, this is where prayer and meditation come in.

2 Peter 1:21" *For prophecy never had its origin in the human will, but prophets, though human, spoke from God as they were carried along by the Holy Spirit."*

Everything that we talked about should lead us to start seeking the guidance of God, through his Holly Spirit.

John 14:16, 17" *And I will ask the Father, and he will give you another advocate to help* *you and be with you forever. The Spirit of truth. The world cannot accept him, because it neither sees him nor knows him. But you know him, for he lives with you and will be in you."*

Every day I ask God to give me the discernment to know when the Holy Spirit is telling me to do something one way or another. Remember, God is going to give you the correct answer. It's okay if you didn't do what the Holy Spirit asked you to do. Maybe at the moment it happened, you didn't realize the Holy Spirit was trying to guide you. It's okay that we made a mistake. The important thing is that you analyzed it and realized afterwards that He was trying to talk to you. Keep seeking His guidance.

Romans 10:17" *Consequently, faith comes from hearing the message, and the message is heard through the word about Christ."*

Addicts who are going through the early stages of recovery really do not have much faith in anyone or anything. Faith is built up through His Word. The mentee has to get to the point where he keeps building his faith. Receiving God's Word is going to build his/her faith and breathe life into them that they need.

John 5:39-40" *You study the Scriptures diligently because you think that in them you have eternal life. These are the very Scriptures that testify about me, yet you refuse to come to me to have life.*"

You have to realize that everything we receive now is because of Jesus. We receive His grace and mercy because of Jesus. We get redemption because of Jesus. We receive a renewed life and increase our faith through the scriptures because of our Lord and Savior Jesus Christ.

2 Timothy 3:15" *and how form infancy you have known the Holy Spirit scriptures, which are able to make you wise for salvation through faith in Jesus Christ.*"

I think one of the biggest advantages we have through the Christian mentorship program is the ability to receive wise biblical counseling. We have access to something that the secular world does not have: God's mind.

Ephesians 3:10" *His intent was that now, through the church, the manifold wisdom of God should be made known to the rulers and authorities in the heavenly realms."*

Romans 15:4" *For everything that was written in the past was written to teach us, so that through the endurance taught in the Scriptures and the encouragement they provide we might have hope."*

God sent His word so that we can learn and use it as a manual. When someone buys a new car, they also get an owner's manual with it. If there is something that you want to figure out how to use in your new car that you do not know how to use, you go to the manual. Even if something is wrong with it, you go to some type of manual and the instructions are there. Most people don't go to the manuals; they either ask someone else or go to the mechanic. Most of us are like that with the bible. God sent us an owner's manual and we really don't use it to try and get to the solution we need with the instructions given to us by God through His work.

1 Peter 4:17" *His intent was that now, through the church, the manifold wisdom of God should be made known to the rulers and authorities in the heavenly realms.*"

One day we are going to be accountable for our actions and how well we listen to God's instruction. We have to encourage each other and remind each other of this and be aware of God's voice.

2 Timothy 3:16"*All Scripture is God-breathed and is useful for teaching, rebuking, correcting and training in righteousness.*"

We have to instruct the mentee on getting a good routine going. Their daily habits have to start including God's Word. God will always have His best intentions for us as long as we seek Him.

Romans 8:28" *And we know that in all things God works for the good of those who love him, who have been called according to his purpose."*

All I know is that I have faith in God and what He will do in my life. I know that He is with me every step of the way. I receive this confidence because I pray, I meditate, I read or listen to the bible, I congregate and I fellowship.

Chapter 8

THROUGH CHRIST OUR PAST IS FORGIVEN

1 John 1:9" *If we confess our sins, he is faithful and just and will forgive us our sins and purify us from all unrighteousness.*"

I think a major factor in a lot of addicts not being able to get through recovery is their feeling of guilt. These feelings might be hidden deep inside of them and purposely unconscious of something that they consciously know and carry with. A lot of addicts do not feel worthy and have low self-esteem. Society as a whole has rejected them. They probably get rejected by friends and family. This rejection is done either inwardly or outwardly, or both. While they are in this stage of addiction they are not in a good place. They most likely take these feelings with them into sobriety. It's probably hard for them realize that there is someone who is willing to completely forget about all the wrong things they did.

Mark 2:5" *When Jesus saw their faith, he said to the paralyzed man, "Son, your sins are forgiven."*

Acts 3:19" *Repent, then, and turn to God, so that your sins may be wiped out, those times of refreshing may come from the Lord."*

The mentee in this process has to know that the sacrifice of Jesus on the Cross was for him also. He has to know this and hold on to it with **OWNERSHIP**. God knew that it is impossible to keep every law. He did not bring the law to tell us what not to do. He brought the law to let His people know what He does not approve of. After Adam there was no other perfect man, until Jesus came, of course Adam failed but we get the point. It was impossible for anyone to follow the law and not sin. God knew all this, in this mentoring process we have to make this mentee realize that God knows the wrong he/she was doing, but that God's love does not depend on that. God is not moved by our bad behavior, he is clear on this in the book of John.

John 3:16" *For God so loved the world that he gave his one and only Son, that whoever believes in him shall not perish but have eternal life."*

We live by grace now and if we have given our life over to Christ and believe that He has given His life for us, and we've confessed our sins and have been cleansed, than we should have nothing to worry about.

2 Corinthians 12:19" *For the Son of God, Jesus Christ, who was preached among you by us—by me and Silas[and Timothy—was not "Yes" and "No," but in him it has always been "Yes."*

2 Corinthians 5:17 *"Therefore, if anyone is in Christ, the new creation has come: The old has gone, the new is here."*

The Apostle Paul brings us all this great news. The mentee should wake up every morning and thank God for this. It became so easy for us after Jesus died. Everything we did, all our transgressions are wiped away in an instant. It's a hard concept to grasp if you don't know Christ, but once you do, you realize that it is possible. All these feelings of guilt and shame, they're supposed to leave also. All of that died on the Cross with Jesus. That's why God put him in charge of us, because he is the one who does this for us. He took us from death to eternal life.

Ephesians 2:8 *"For it is by grace you have been saved, through faith—and this is not from yourselves, it is the gift of God."*

All born again Christians live by grace. Other people might want to put other burdens on us, but that's not what the bible tells me.

Ephesians 1:7 "In him we have redemption through his blood, the forgiveness of sins, in accordance with the riches of God's grace."

I remember when I got out of prison and I was on parole. I had to go see my parole officer every week or once a month, I don't remember. I would see some of the guys I used to hang out with or that I was in incarcerated with. We would greet each other and talk for a little bit. They were my friends. A lot of them I knew personally and had hung out with them at one time or another. The parole officer would see me talking to them and ask if I knew them, we were not really supposed to be associating together because those were the rules of being on parole. The parole officer would ask me if I really knew those guys and what they had done. He would say that they really were not good people. I would tell the parole agent that I realized he had paper work that said my friends were bad people but that I knew them differently. I told him that I knew my friends personally and that they were good people and that they had a good heart. God looks at us this way. God is looking at our heart and the changes He can make there. He knows our potential and what we are capable where others don't see it.

Titus 3:7" *so that, having been justified by his grace, we might become heirs having the hope of eternal life."*

Hebrews 10:17, 18"Then he adds: "Their sins and lawless acts

I will remember no more." And where these have been forgiven, sacrifice for sin."

With Jesus in our life, our past is not something that we should carry. Being on drugs, sometimes you accept that people look down on you. It becomes normal to you that you are not looked at with respect. Living that type of life out in the streets, there is no self-respect for human life. It's a whole different world where you see entire families hooked on drugs, I remember I used to sell drugs on this certain street in Philadelphia. I used to see this one kid who was 15 and hooked on heroin, I saw another who was homeless and hooked on crack. There was a lady hooked on crack also. There was a crack house that they used to go to. I didn't know until afterwards that they were all related. She was the mother and they were her two kids. We all walked past them and never knew them or realized that they were a family. This family just accepted the fact that they were drug addicts and that nobody paid any attention to them or had any respect for them. They accepted it as normal life. I don't know if they knew Jesus back then.

Hebrew 4:16" *Let us then approach God's throne of grace with confidence, so that we may receive mercy and find grace to help us in our time of need."*

Daniel 9:9" *The Lord our God is merciful and forgiving, even though we have rebelled against him."*

James 4:6" *But he gives us more grace. That is why Scripture say "God opposes the proud but shows favor to the humble."*

The mentee at this point is starting to be molded and shaped into what God wants him to be. God wants him/her to be Free in Christ. He wants to give him/her Favor. Throughout this process we must maintain a humble approach. There is a balance that we have to keep. The mentee should be mature enough at this stage.

Isaiah 6:3" *And they were calling to one another: "Holy, holy, holy is the LORD Almighty; the whole earth is full of his glory."*

Everything that goes on in this process is for God's glory. It should always be our goal. Our rewards should not be His glory. His glory is His glory.

Colossians 1:13, 14 "For he has rescued us from the dominion of darkness and brought us into the kingdom of the Son he loves, in whom we have redemption, the forgiveness of sins."

Every time a mentee has a thought about his/her past or they hear someone bringing up the past, remember that Jesus Christ paid the price for all that. We should always keep that in mind.

Psalm 103:12" *as far as the east is from the west,*

so far has he removed our transgressions from us."

I sometimes think about the pain and destruction I caused my family, and it's not because I feel guilty. I think about it because I never want to make the same mistake again. Believe me, I know I did wrong. I don't feel guilt or shame about the past because Jesus made sure I don't have to. Everything is put on the Cross.

John 3:17-18" *For God did not send his Son into the world to condemn the world, but to save the world through him. Whoever believes in him is not condemned, but whoever does not believe stands condemned already because they have not believed in the name of God's one and only Son.*"

Titus 2:11" *For the grace of God has appeared that offers salvation to all people.*"

Chapter 9

THE FEAR OF GOD

Proverbs 1:17" *The fear of the LORD is the beginning of knowledge, but fools despise wisdom and instruction."*

King Solomon brought up the "fear of the Lord" many times in the book of Proverbs. I read at least nine of them. I think that it's important for the mentee to realize that this verse right here is what is going to keep him sober. Fear of the Lord is where you are going to realize that without Him, you can't do anything. I think the verse and the phrase is not used correctly by most people all the time. It's not a sentence that is meant to intimidate you. It has nothing to do with emotional feelings. God is not trying to get at your emotions.

He is not trying to play psychological games with you. "Fear of the Lord "is a realization and an understanding, that without God, you are nothing. That's why Solomon mentions that it is the beginning of "knowledge". It's your intellect that He's trying to stimulate, not your emotions.

Proverbs 8:13" *To fear the LORD is to hate evil; I hate pride and arrogance, evil behavior and perverse speech."*

This knowledge and wisdom that Solomon received is something we should study on a regular basis. The mentor and mentee have to be more aware and more in tune with this atmosphere that we are surrounded by. Our intellect and discernment that we receive is where God is going to help guide us through our process. God doesn't want us to just be followers. He wants us to think and utilize the Scriptures to get us through our everyday lives. God was so happy that Solomon asked for wisdom that He just gave him wealth and fame also.

Ephesians 6:12" *For our struggle is not against flesh and blood, but against the rulers, against the authorities, against the powers of this dark world and against the spiritual forces of evil in the heavenly realms."*

You have to keep building this knowledge and <u>wisdom is your defense system.</u>

Ephesians 6:11" *Put on the full armor of God, so that you can take your stand against the devil's schemes."*

I think that the "fear of God" is something that is not embraced because it's a commitment, and people have the wrong perception on this term. The fear of God is something that should be embraced and it's vital to our Life in Christ.

Proverbs 1:29" *since they hated knowledge and did not choose to fear the LORD."*

I think that the cause of most of the Christians who stop serving God, is the lack of a fear in God. A lot of Christians stay distant from God or stop going to church because other Christians drove them away from church or hurt them. I think that if you have the true fear of God in you, you will forget about what those other Christians did to you and start asking God to take you back and find another church. I don't really believe that you should be jumping from church to church, but maybe, sometimes it's necessary to find another church. God is not involved the business of feelings and emotions. Our God is a God of truth. The truth doesn't always please people, but what matters most is what God says.

Proverbs 9:10" *The fear of the LORD is the beginning of wisdom and knowledge of the Holy One is understanding."*

Proverbs 2:1-5" *My son, if you accept my words and store up my commands within you, turning your ear to wisdom and applying your heart to understanding— indeed, if you call out for insight and cry aloud for understanding,* *and if you look for it as for silver and search for it as for hidden treasure, then you will understand the fear of the LORD and find the knowledge of God."*

The fear of God is important to the mentorship program because if the mentee does not have the fear of God, there is a big problem. Not fearing God is an easy way for the mentee to fail. Knowing that God is in control of everything is what is going to get you through a successful mentorship.

Joshua 1:5" *No one will be able to stand against you all the days of your life. As I was with Moses, so I will be with you; I will never leave you nor forsake you."*

God is sovereign over everything, especially if you let Him take over your life.

Psalms 103:19" *The LORD has established his throne in heaven, and his kingdom rules over all."*

The fear of God establishes a discipline in your life. There is no emotional fear in this, only comprehension of God being in control of your life.

Proverbs 14:26" *Whoever fears the LORD has a secure fortress,*

and for their children it will be a refuge."

Proverbs 15:13" *A happy heart makes the face cheerful,*

but heartache crushes the spirit."

There was a time in my life where I was at my worst. I was doing drugs and doing alcohol and isolating myself. I was getting to a very dark place in my life. It got to the point where I was so deep into the darkness that I actually saw demons. I still remember to this day vividly the demons in front of me. I was so caught up in my lifestyle that even this did not make me stop. Bringing the fear of God into my way of thinking was the only thing that made me want to never go back to the point where I was.

Proverbs 14:27." *The fear of the LORD is a fountain of life,*

turning a person from the snares of death"

2 chronicles 19:9 *"Repent, then, and turn to God, so that your sins may be wiped out, those times of refreshing may come from the Lord, and that he may send the Messiah."*

I remember one day I was on a drug corner in the streets of Philadelphia. It was it was after midnight some time. I do not remember. I was selling cocaine to some people. All of a sudden I hear someone calling my name from above. I looked up and thought someone way calling me from one of the apartments above, but I didn't see any one. Then whoever was calling me finally said "Francis I'm up here in the tree." I looked up and saw my friend David up high in the tree. He was wearing a mask. I asked him what he was doing up in the tree, wearing the mask. He said "when I use drugs with the mask up here in the tree, it makes it feel better." David had no fear of using drugs, high up in a tree where he could fall and die. Right attitude, wrong concept. If we could take that fearless attitude and apply it to serving God, we can't fail.

Job 28:28 *"And he said to the human race, "The fear of the Lord—that is wisdom, and to shun evil understands."*

Psalms 19:9" *The fear of the LORD is pure, enduring forever. The decrees of the LORD are firm, and all of them are righteous."*

Fear of the God is something that has to be learned. It's a process. If you don't have it, you should seek after it. The mentee should start thinking that God will make the changes to his/her life that are necessary to better his/her life. God wants to be involved. Sometimes we just don't let him. I think we unconsciously feel we don't need God In certain aspects of our lives. I really think this is where fear of the Lord changes that way of thinking. I think we sub-consciously omit God from the equation. Fear of God changes that into making a conscious effort to include Him in the equation.

Proverbs 31:30" *Charm is deceptive, and beauty is fleeting;*

but a woman who fears the LORD is to be praised."

There is no exact formula to try to gain Fear of the Lord. It's just something that you consciously have to keep striving for, just like king Solomon tells us:

Proverbs 1:7" *The fear of the LORD is the beginning of knowledge, but fools despise wisdom and instruction.*"

Genesis 20:11" *Abraham replied, "I said to myself, 'There is surely no fear of God in this place, and they will kill me because of my wife.*"

Abraham was consciously aware that these people had no fear of the Lord, and he wanted no part of them. In other words if he had told them the truth about Sarah, they might take action without worrying about the consequences. God had to interfere by giving this King a dream. The mentee has to start acquiring that discernment, just like Abraham did. It was vital for Abraham keeping himself and his family alive and it's vital for the mentee to keep himself and his family alive as well.

CONCLUSION

Christian Mentorship is something that could potentially revive entire families, neighborhoods or cities. These recovering addicts are exactly the same type of people David would have taken with him when he was hiding from Saul in the cave.

1 Samuel 22:1, 2" David left Gath and escaped to the cave of Adullam. When his brothers and his father's household heard about it, they went down to him there. All those who were in distress or in debt or discontented gathered around him, and he became their commander. About four hundred men were with him."

These broken men and women are waiting anxiously for Christian Mentors out there to take the time to get them through these very delicate moments in their recovery. Christian Mentorship works, but it takes time. There are not a lot of people that are willing to take this challenge. There are so many people in need.

Matthew 9:37 *"Then he said to his disciples, "The harvest is plentiful but the workers are few."*

These sons of God that are waiting to be mentored have a uniqueness that God needs to expand His Kingdom. We should all be a part of that.

REFERENCES

- Scripture taken from the Holy Bible, New International Version.
- Internet article on OAS was taken from the webpage;
  Cicad.oas.org January 2013
- The blog on Reverend Dr. Paul Bradley was taken from;
  Regator.com September 2011
- Internet article on recovery clinics in Mexico was taken from;
  Foxnews.com June 2012

GLOSSARY

- CICAD.OAS.ORG
- FOXNEWS.COM
- HOLY BIBLE, NEW INTERNATIONAL VERSION 1973 ZONDERVAN REGATOR.COM

www.ingramcontent.com/pod-product-compliance
Ingram Content Group UK Ltd.
Pitfield, Milton Keynes, MK11 3LW, UK
UKHW041944230426
12048UKWH00008B/129